THE

FOUNTAIN;

WITH

JETS OF NEW MEANINGS.

Illustrated with One Hundred and Forty-Two Engravings

BY

ANDREW JACKSON DAVIS.

"There's a fount about to stream,
There's a light about to gleam."

THIRD EDITION.

BOSTON:
WILLIAM WHITE & COMPANY,
BANNER OF LIGHT OFFICE, 158 WASHINGTON STREET.
NEW YORK:
AMERICAN NEWS CO., AGENTS, 119 NASSAU STREET.
1871.

INTRODUCTION.

One bright morning last May, as I was idly sleeping at the foot of a grand mountain, the voice of a revered instructor said: "Arise! Go up to the very top; survey the ways of wisdom; observe the needs of the world; be healthful and hopeful, and perform thy work."

After journeying through a mass of chilly clouds, which clung to the steep sides of the mountain, I gained the glorious summit. With serene joy and grateful admiration, I gazed upon the magnificence of the heavens, and upon the loveliness of the earth, which were unfolded and displayed in every direction. And observing no human being near me, and feeling myself alone in the lofty solitudes of the mountain, I turned toward mankind, and said: "O world! here am I, after a slow and toilsome progress, far away from you, yet ready to work for you. What will you accept from me?"

And suddenly there appeared in the beautiful landscape, not far from the foot of the mountain, A FOUNTAIN! It was exceedingly beautiful in its strength and simplicity. The sparkling water was flowing and jetting incessantly. And the waters of that Fountain seemed to be compounded of the *needs* and *wants* and *wishes* of multitudes, yea, hundreds of thousands, of warm, living human hearts!

And in the beautiful light above the fount, a friendly voice said: "Write a book, with thoughts for men and pictures for children, which the young as well as the matured can peruse with pleasure and profit." After a silence, the voice added: "Truth, Love, Peace, Mercy, Wisdom, Labor, Education, Religion, Admonition, Hope—these streams, with occasional jets and clear intimations of new meanings, must flow from the Fountain. To this end employ little things. With pure affections and familiar illustrations you must appeal to the understanding and the heart. To improve the human mind, and to aid and enliven the world's mothers and fathers and educators, you must amuse while you instruct."

Accordingly, in obedience to the voice of wisdom, I proceeded to "write," and the present volume is the result.

Employing every aid at my command, I have attempted, with the utmost sincerity of motive, to relieve the grave profundities and the dazzling magnitude of the Harmonial Ideas, by the introduction of pleasing simplicities which may attract and instruct persons of every age and in all states of feeling. And all deficiencies, as well as the omission of many deeply important subjects, must be attributed to the fact that this volume is designed to be simply the first of a short series of like import. In this book there is no effort to sound the very *deep* in the treatment of any question. The wish to attract and enlighten young persons—in short, to reach the entire family group—is paramount to the desire to impart original ideas to established thinkers.

"I have often thought," remarks a scholarly writer, "if the minds of men were laid open, we should see but little difference between that of a wise man, and that of a fool. There are infinite reveries, numberless extravagances, and a succession of vanities, which pass through each." Of grown-up men and women, and of little children and our young folks, the same reflection seems to be not less applicable. Whatever is truly attractive, pleasing, and instructive to one is likely to be equally entertaining and profitable to the other. It has thus far been observed that, among the hundreds of thousands of elderly persons who drink deeply and constantly at the Harmonial Fountains, not more than a few score of young people read and enjoy our publications and principles.

If the flowings of this Fountain shall have the effect to attract and instruct young persons, while slacking the honest thirst of the grave and thoughtful, and if the teachings of this initial volume shall in some degree assist parents and tutors in the rearing and just education of children, the Author will deem his industry amply rewarded. And he will interpret the general acceptance of this work to mean that additional books in this series are called for.

A. J. DAVIS.

NEW YORK, September 20, 1870.

CONTENTS.

I.

The Everlasting O.

THE English alphabet contains no letter more remarkable than the familiar fourth vowel, O; with which, therefore, I have elected to begin this book of interior entertainments.

The fifteenth letter is written and spoken more frequently than any other in the language, with the exception of the superlatively important initial, A. This is because no other letter so spontaneously expresses the many and various feelings of the impressible spirit. It involuntarily bubbles up to the tongue, in the shape of an interjection, as the natural sound of almost every imaginable emotion—of surprise, joy, alarm, aversion, sorrow, supplication.

Bees do not swarm more thickly into a clover-field than does this letter crowd itself into the flowers of literature. The very existence of poetry depends upon the existence of this simple vowel. Starting with these hints, where can you not go in tracing the indispensability of this item of the alphabet? The entire structure of literature would crumble should one letter be withdrawn. Thus we learn, that least things are necessary to the greatest.

Let us remember, right here, that the first and the last letters in the Greek alphabet are A and O. Hence, in the Bible phraseology, the representative terms, "Alpha and Omega," are naturally used to signify the beginning and the end.

A is the first figure employed to symbolize the first vocal sound made irresistibly by merely opening the mouth, with the feeling or wish of utterance in the heart. A, M, and O come out of the sweet lips of infants as naturally as music flows from the mouths of birds.

Destroy the letter O, and you annihilate the Greek language. And then, what would become of poetry and prayers? "O heart of fire!" tell us what would be thy fate? Men of language! tell us who, deprived of the use of this letter, could exclaim "O, Lord!" "O, Mother Church!" "O, God, Omnipotent!" Without the sound of O, there could be no natural expression in any language of the emotions of joy, warning, admiration, entreaty, or compassion. In vain might we hunt for a substitute

"Over low-lands forest-grown,
Over waters island-strown,
Over silver-sanded beach;"

yet, forever, a better letter would be beyond our reach; therefore, O vowel, wisely chosen! we lovingly cling to thee through the flower-fields of literature, through the quiet aisles of prayer; yea, through the never-ebbing sea of immortal love we will cling to thee! Without this letter, the following could not exist in any language:

"For the sound of waters gushing
In bubbling beads of light;
For the fleets of snow-white lilies—
Firm anchors out of sight;
For the reeds among the eddies—
The crystal on the clod;
For the flowing of the rivers,
We thank thee, oh, our God!

"For the lifting up of mountains
In brightness and in dread;
For the peaks where snow and sunshine
Alone have dared to tread;
For the dark of silent gorges
Whence giant cedars nod,
For the majesty of mountains,
We thank thee, oh, our God!

"For an eye of inward seeing—
A soul to know and love;
For these common aspirations
Which our high heirship prove;
For the tokens of thy presence
Within, above, abroad;
For thine own great gift of being,
We thank thee, oh, our God!"

What a history of completeness and perfection is the history of this simple figure, O. About three hundred and fifty years before the era of Christianity, Plato began the investigation of the circle. After two centuries of researches by different spiritual philosophers into the elements of the circle—the ellipse being one of the conic sections—the figure remained without further analysis for over sixteen hundred years. O how long! At length, however, the remarkable properties of our letter were brought to light through minute mathematical investigation.

Although this book is not designed to deal in philosophical abstractions, it cannot be deemed inappropriate to quote a passage from the wise and comprehensive writer, J. W. Jackson, of Glasgow, who, being a faithful spiritual philosopher, perceives and affirms the spiritual origin of forms and figures. In the London magazine entitled *Human Nature*, for June, 1870, he thus comprehensively describes angles, circles, and the ellipse: "The primordial bodies on the cosmic plane—suns, planets, and their satellites—are spherical, because the sphere or universal circle represents the perfection of a unitary totality, whereof they are the primal reflection and reproduction. The circle in process of formation represents creation in evolution. When closed, by the movement of the radius vector over the entire cyclical circuit, it equally represents creation finished, and so ready for reabsorption into the Divine unity. We thus see that the centre symbolizes Deity and the circumference creation, the radius vector being a projection of the Divine, from the eternal sphere of the

Infinite ONE to the temporal plane of the finite many, or as the mystics would say, God in manifestation as the Demiurgus, or Logos Creator.

"As the sphere or universal circle represents completeness and perfection, so the cube or universal square represents equipoise and strength, and thus morally symbolizes justice and power. It is in every direction equilateral, and thus all its angles are right angles. It is the symbol of being as based on truth and rectitude. As the sphere, or universal circle, is representative of the unity, so the cube, or universal square, is symbolical of the trinity of form—that is, of height, length, and breadth, equal in dimension, yet diverse in direction; that is again, as the mystics would say, co-ordinate in rank, equal in power, yet different in function. The sphere represents those divine integers, eternity and infinity, having neither beginning nor end; while the cube or universal square, on the contrary, symbolizes time and space, each susceptible of the most rigid limitation—the sequences of the former implying definite periods of duration; and the expanses of the latter limited areas of extension, like the lines and sides of a cube. Perhaps the reader begins now to understand something of the Pythagorean reverence for numbers, and the belief once prevalent, as to the magical power of mathematical diagrams.

"The circle—and with it, of course, the sphere—is masculine because it is unitary, being formed on one centre, and generated by the movement of one radius vector. *An ellipse*, on the contrary, *is feminine*, being formed on two foci, whose distance is the test of its feminity, the intervening area being the sphere of multiplicity. So a square, or cube, is masculine, while a parallelogram, or parallelopiped, is feminine, the continent lines of length transcending those of breadth or height, so that it is no longer the symbol of absolute rectitude, strength, or stability. It may, perhaps, also be observed, that both in the ellipse and the parallelogram the containing lines are longer in proportion to the area enclosed than in the circle and the square."

A perfect O—which is feminine—is a perfect ellipse. It is the most harmonious mathematical figure, containing all the lines and curves and elements of beauty; and it is the form of the orbits traversed by the planets of space. Without the O, the universally useful "multiplication table" would be an impossibility. Because, without this plain, frank letter to stand with its great meaning upon the right hand of other figures, we could never make any progress beyond the figure 9.

Therefore was I not doing right to begin this little volume with the essential symbol of a yet more essential part of being? It is a key in every hand.

My pen needs but the prefix O, to empower it to "open" before you many pioneer paths leading through great mountains "of new meanings."

SAILING OUT TO FIND NEW MEANINGS.

Now let each reader choose his favorite keel, with which to plough the sea of spiritual commerce and intellectual discovery. Every sailor will feel most at home on his own vessel. If you would sail out upon life's wide ocean—if you would search the winter lands of earth while on your great voyage to summer lands, among the golden stars and beneath clearer skies on high—then enlist at once as helmsman upon the best ship now riding in the harbor of your own honest knowledge.

SAILOR'S OCEAN HOME.

"O lonely Bay of Trinity,
O dreary shores, give ear!
Lean down unto the white-lipped sea
The voice of God to hear."

But let all remember humility; without O, you cannot sail your ship far *out*; indeed, without it you cannot even weigh anchor. Who ever tried to write anchor without the use of the fifteenth letter?

AN HONEST MIND IS AN ANCHOR TO THE SOUL.

Very sweet and liquid is the sturdy-looking half-vowel, M! It is, I freely confess, quite as necessary to Latin as O is to Greek. But being one of the easiest to articulate, M is likely to be the first upon the rosy lips of childhood. It comes, O so sweetly! in the first utterance of "ma." And yet, somehow, I cannot yield the assertion that our chosen feminine ellipse is the sovereign letter. You cannot perfectly articulate M, except while closing your mouth and compressing the lips. Now, to try an experiment, step before your mirror and pronounce the beautiful letter under consideration. O what a fair countenance you present! What an "open" mouth you immediately possess! Therefore, sustained by such prime-facial evidence, I dare affirm that M is by nature contractive and conservative; while our beautiful O is expansive, and maketh the mouth ready to speak from "the abundance of the heart."

An Oasis, without the letter O, is impossible. The Libyan deserts of human life—without ever-green spots, and without fountains of musical waters—would destroy mankind. "Orpheus," without our opening letter, with all his miracles of music, would drop out of the world. As suddenly would vanish from the world's romantic literature the name "Ossian," the son of Fingal; and thus, too, would forever disappear "Orion," and the great universe of constellations would know him no more.

And, let me ask, what would become of the Ottoman Empire? It would require a greater than the renowned Oberlin to portray the scenes accompanying the downfall of the house of Orleans. The lovely images and picturesque expressions of Ovid, with all his pathos, would vanish in an instant, as would also the great agitator, O'Connell, and the innumerable "O's" which mean so much as a prefix to names of persons in the old, unhappy land. And unspeakably learned Oxford would sink into the place appointed unto all unprogressive institutions.

Did you ever reflect that, without the fourth vowel, the revered name of "God" could not be written; that, if deprived of this talismanic letter, we could not print the sacred words "mother," "love," "home;" that, without it, as if crushed by a thunder-bolt, all life would suddenly be deprived of its "glory;" and that, without it, the idea of an eternal "morning" could never succeed to the night and gloom of existence?

A great, strong anchor, both sure and steadfast, we therefore find in the perfect ellipse—our initial letter O! Even the name of goodness is impossible without it; yet, happily, the *state* of goodness is independent of all speech.

COLD! AND, O SO DREARY.

Politicians profoundly realize the value of this vowel while laboring for Office, and especially when called upon to "take the Oath." Lawyers depend upon the fifteenth letter when orally opening cases —the outlines of which, together with the order of the offence, with objects, observations, obtruding obstacles, optional or otherwise—thus they read and define the oblong character on the obelisks of legal lore and sail out upon the broad ocean of ownership.

"O PRINCELY LOT! O BLISSFUL ART!"

And of Clergymen—what can we say? "O ye of little faith!" From over the old ocean of ancient usages the office of the ministers of the "Holy One" has been brought to the shores of the new continent. And by virtue of that office, and especially owing to the endorsements of custom, the clergyman is a wholesale dealer in the most sacred feelings, emotions, and passions of the human breast. His language in prayer is therefore habitually interjectional. "How long, O Lord, how long" shall this style of expression continue? is a question not yet answered. The templed mountain of Olympus does not more truly o'ertop the valleys than do the churches of to-day attempt to outrank the testimonies of Nature. While the office of minister remains, the frequent and untrammelled pronunciation of "O" must also remain, and must be unfeignedly respected by all who sincerely believe in ministers.

Imagine just here, O friendly reader! the hundreds of thousands of words from which the letter O cannot be for one instant omitted. Recall the phrases which awaken no agreeable emotions. Are they not northerly and extremely cold words? Do they not come breathing forth the chilly electricities of the frozen Hebrides? Northerly and exquisitely bitter words, freighted with st*o*rm and sn*o*w and fr*o*st—with which thoughts and feelings of l*o*neliness and des*o*lation are tearfully intermingled. For even so sounds, in the chambers of my inner hearing, all phrases not flowing from the fountain of wisdom and love.

Language, like the wave of a magician's wand, can suddenly transform every thing about us. Because spirit is the fountain of feeling and wishes, and is, therefore, the cause of words spoken by the obedient tongue.

Let us, therefore, avoid, as far as possible, the articulation of words which casts "sweet home" into the dim and distant background of life's picture. Let us never employ any language which would hang our master-letter upon the scraggy limbs of some fruitless tree—upon some leafless tree of materialistic knowledge.

II.

Beauty and Destiny of Mother Nature's Darlings.

FATHER GOD calls to His children. He calls them not through the bending domes and crumbling arches of stone churches built with mortal hands. But His fatherly voice comes through the suns and stars of the boundless firmament; through the stately monuments and constellations of the universe; through the swerveless laws of the stupendous whole; through the love-breathings of the interior heart; through the starry corridors of the eternal temple of Truth; through the winds and waves of innumerable oceans; through the cathedral solitudes and ineffable perfections of Nature.

Godless, indeed, is that religion which would silence (or rate as *beneath* paper books) the voices of such living bibles and perpetual preachers as fruit-trees, wild flowers, beautiful birds, whispering bees, sobbing seas, sighing winds, snow-covered mountains, and the grand old pines and mighty oaks bending with the weight and majesty of centuries.

"Were I in churchless solitudes remaining;
Free from all voice of churchmen or divines,
My soul would find in flowers of God's ordaining,
Priests, sermons, shrines."

Rightly seen, every thing in nature is a wise and special expression of divine affection. Indians and children and poets, when in their best moods, see the Father-Spirit in every place and in all manifestations. Merrily sings the divine love in birds and bees and blossoms. And sadly sings the Infinite Spirit through the dark-green branches of mountain pines, and in the unutterable sounds of the ebbing and flowing sea. Infallibly speaks the Eternal in the boundlessness and unchangeability of those invisible principles by which all things live and move and have their being.

LOVE AND LABOR AMONG FLOWERS OF GOD'S ORDAINING.

Nature is God's conjugal mate; she is, therefore, the Mother of All. Children, like young birds, feel in their hearts the life of heavenly liberty. Girls not less than boys long for the delights of the wide, open fields and far-spreading trees. Boys, naturally, more than girls, seek bold and boisterous sports. Girls are taught to seek and personate the graceful, to dwell modestly in the quiet retirements, and to cultivate the noiseless, the impractical, and the beautiful. This teaching is founded in the belief that girls are by nature finer than boys. While the truth is, they are only exact counterparts, reversed; each qualitatively and in substance like the other; but from exactly opposite sides of the universe. They are born of the same mother, nourished at the same fountain, clothed by the same hand, reared in the same home, watched over by the same guardian angels, pass through the process of death upon the same safe principles, and journey to brighter and fairer lands upon the same celestial highway.

But a false system of religion, which is as arbitrary as the old fable which discriminates and establishes an antagonism between sheep and goats, has come between children and their intuitions of truth.

The beautiful butterfly, which used to represent the idea of individual life after death, attracts the girl by its beauty and the boy as an object of pursuit. Girls and boys are drawn into the fields by the same healthy, sensuous attractions. While sisters gather blooming buttercups, their brothers chase the fleeting butterflies; but after

BOYS ARE INFLUENCED BY THE BEAUTIFUL.

government, when they attain to the estate of men and women? Why not? Because a false religion, feeding and flattering a false custom, insists peremptorily, with terrible penalties of excommunication from "good society," that girls shall forever dress unlike boys, shall studiously refrain from running and climbing, shall make no visible demonstrations of bodily vigor, and shall do nothing and be nothing inconsistent with the established masculine rules of feminine propriety.

The dress of a girl is constructed so that it is certain to trammel her limbs, pervert her growth, derange the functions of the bodily organs, and in truth endanger the safety of her physical existence. Her younger brother can freely and fearlessly climb hillsides, race through the wildwoods, leap fences, and play like other darlings on the bosom of Nature. But only dare to let her go out with her brother, and lo! owing to her dress, she falls headlong over the straight gate of pharisaical propriety, and is "providentially saved," if her beautiful life is not forever crushed against the rocks of a blind and bigoted custom.

LET HER FOLLOW THE FASHIONS.

the mediums through which the man-organization makes itself manifest, are aggressive in their very nature. And yet it should be borne in mind that some women are in this respect equal, if not superior, to some men; but habits and education, as much as temperament and sex, have great sway in determining the manifestations of any personality. Habits exert a subtle influence. Women, especially among the ancient Romans, by systematically educating their muscles, and by abstaining from all intoxicating drinks, developed noble mothers and a hardy race of sons. The Romans were famous for their health, strength, and endurance. It is safe to say that Roman and Spartan mothers were physically stronger and more enduring than many of the men and fathers in our more refined era.

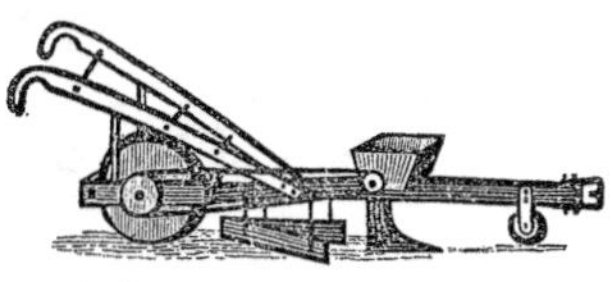

A PLAN FOR COMPELLING THE EARTH TO ACCEPT SEED.

Still, there is a constitutional difference between a woman-nature and a man-nature which lies deeper than any habits or circumstances—a difference which, although absolute and essential, is not necessarily antagonistic. This sex-difference was illustrated by Mr. R. Grant White, in an account he somewhere published, in substance, as follows: "Some years ago, before monitors or even iron-clad ships were thought of, the enormous and now utterly useless man-of-war *Pennsylvania* lay at the Washington navy-yard. Much had been expected of her, and her colossal size, and her enormous battery of one hundred and twenty guns, were looked upon with pride by all 'true Americans.' It was determined that the President of the United States, accompanied by the members of his Cabinet, the principal officers of the army and navy, and other persons of like distinction, should visit her for an 'inaugural' entertainment, and that in honor of the occasion, he and they should be saluted by the discharge of all her guns. The gentlemen were accompanied by a large number of ladies, and a more numerous and representative party was probably never gathered together on the decks of a national vessel. The salute began, and the rapid discharge of the heavy ordnance produced a remarkable effect on the civilian visitors. Very soon the men were stunned or worried, and showed strong symptoms of nervous anxiety. The women, on the contrary, to the surprise of all, showed no fear, but rather delight, and were cheerfully excited, not concealing an inclination to laugh at and crow over the nervous weakness of their masculine companions. The firing went on, and became a protracted and apparently endless series of regular explosions. For the discharge of one hundred and twenty guns at intervals of only three seconds occupies six minutes, measured by three-second counts, even in silence, seem as if they would never end. But when, as in this case, each interval is marked by a roar that stuns the ears and a concussion that shakes the heavens and the earth, and fills the air with flame and smoke, the performance becomes oppressive and tries nervous endurance to the utmost. And on this occasion a striking natural phenomenon, full of moral significance, was presented to the curious student of human nature. It was observed that as gun followed gun, the men, who were so disturbed at first, became quiet, self-possessed, indifferent, and at last cheerful, while the women, who at first were so filled with life and gayety, soon showed signs of weariness, then of nervous excitement, and finally of terror, looking forward with dread to the inevitable and regularly-recurring shock; so that before the salute was over most of them were in a state of extreme distress, some were hysterical and some had fainted. Their nerves could bound with elasticity at a single fillip, but succumbed under repeated blows; while the masculine nature toughened under resistance to the protracted strain."

The difference between the man-temperaments and the woman-temperaments, is forcibly illustrated in the foregoing incident.

The man-temperament (which is sometimes also

A MILL FOR CRUSHING AND PULVERIZING.

strong wagons for carrying lumber, stone, and iron; at the steamboats for riding rivers, lakes, and oceans; at the railroads and locomotives made to accomplish Jupiter-like labor; at the wire paths for lightning under oceans and around the great globe! And think, too, of the discovery and settlement of new countries.

These tools, these ambitions, these achievements, these broad and mighty enterprises, are crowded by mother Nature into the restless hearts and into the incessantly pleading hands of her children—into the open hands and prayerful hearts of women and men alike—and then only time and circumstances, and the spirit's faithfulness to its own interior convictions, can determine which sex, and what particular individuals among men and women, are most attracted and adapted to the grand ends and uses in contemplation.

MEANS AND ENDS.

Man's force-and-drive elements combine naturally and fruitfully with woman's elements of power-and-

www.ingramcontent.com/pod-product-compliance
Lightning Source LLC
LaVergne TN
LVHW021252110826
845151LV00005BA/1500